South Dakota

BY ANN HEINRICHS

Content Adviser: Pam Chamberlain, Children's Services Coordinator, South Dakota State Library, Pierre, South Dakota

Reading Adviser: Dr. Linda D. Labbo, Department of Reading Education, College of Education, The University of Georgia

Gainesboro Elementary School
Winchester, Virginia

COMPASS POINT BOOKS MINNEAPOLIS, MINNESOTA

Compass Point Books
3109 West 50th Street, #115
Minneapolis, MN 55410

Visit Compass Point Books on the Internet at *www.compasspointbooks.com*
or e-mail your request to *custserv@compasspointbooks.com*

On the cover: Buffalo in Wind Cave National Park

Photographs ©: Brian Parker/Tom Stack & Associates, cover, 1; PhotoDisc, 3, 8, 10 (bottom),
22, 43 (top), 44 (bottom), 45; Photo Network/Patti McConville, 5; Photo Network/Grace Davies, 6;
Hulton/Archive by Getty Images, 9, 12, 15, 30, 46; Digital Stock, 10 (top), 42; Steve Mulligan
Photography, 11; North Wind Picture Archives, 13, 16, 18; Getty Images, 17, 41; Corbis/Bettmann,
19, 21; Unicorn Stock Photos/Paula J. Harrington, 20; Unicorn Stock Photos/Eric R. Berndt, 23, 27;
Marquette University, 25; Bill Webster/Visuals Unlimited, 26; Corbis/Peter Johnson, 28; Corbis/
AFP, 29; Photo by South Dakota Tourism, 31, 47; Photo by South Dakota Tourism/Chad Coppess
Photography, 32, 48 (top); Unicorn Stock Photos/Chuck Schweiser, 33; David Falconer, 34; John Elk
III, 35, 37, 40; Unicorn Stock Photos/Karen Holsinger Mullen, 38; Robesus, Inc., 43 (state flag); One
Mile Up, Inc., 43 (state seal); Unicorn Stock Photos/Ted Rose, 44 (top); Spencer Swanger/Tom Stack
& Associates, 44 (middle).

Editors: E. Russell Primm, Emily J. Dolbear, and Patricia Stockland
Photo Researcher: Marcie C. Spence
Photo Selector: Linda S. Koutris
Designer: The Design Lab
Cartographer: XNR Productions, Inc.

Library of Congress Cataloging-in-Publication Data
Heinrichs, Ann.
  South Dakota / by Ann Heinrichs.
      p. cm. — (This land is your land)
Includes bibliographical references (p.) and index.
Contents: Welcome to South Dakota!—Hills, badlands, and plains—A trip through time—
Government by the people—South Dakotans at work—Getting to know South Dakotans—Let's
explore South Dakota!
  ISBN 0-7565-0286-1
1. South Dakota—Juvenile literature. [1. South Dakota.] I. Title. II. Series.
  F651.3 .H45 2003
  978.3—dc21   2002012868

Table of Contents

NOTE: In this book, words that are defined in the glossary are in **bold** *the first time they appear in the text.*

"Let us place there, carved high, as close to heaven as we can, the [faces] of our leaders. . . . Then breathe a prayer that these records will endure until the wind and the rain alone shall wear them away."

Gutzon Borglum was proud as he spoke these words. He carved gigantic faces into South Dakota's Mount Rushmore. They represent four great U.S. presidents—George Washington, Thomas Jefferson, Abraham Lincoln, and Theodore Roosevelt. Borglum believed this **monument** stood for America's ideals. Before long, people called it the Shrine of Democracy. South Dakota's nickname became the Mount Rushmore State.

South Dakota is known for many other sites, as well. The Black Hills are filled with natural beauty. They have forests, waterfalls, canyons, and caves. The Badlands are a stark expanse of strange rock formations.

South Dakota's Sioux people gave the state its name. Their word *Dakota* means "friends" or "allies." South

▲ Spearfish Canyon is an example of South Dakota's natural beauty.

Dakotans are proud of their state. They share its beauty and welcome visitors as friends. Now let's see all they have to share.

Hills, Badlands, and Plains

South Dakota lies in the north-central part of the country. It's almost a perfect rectangle, or box-shaped figure. Montana and Wyoming are on the west. To the east are Minnesota and Iowa. Nebraska lies to the south. To the north lies North Dakota, of course!

The Missouri River cuts South Dakota in two. Land east of the Missouri is called East River. Farmers grow corn, hay, and

▲ Roam Free Park along the banks of the Missouri River near Chamberlain

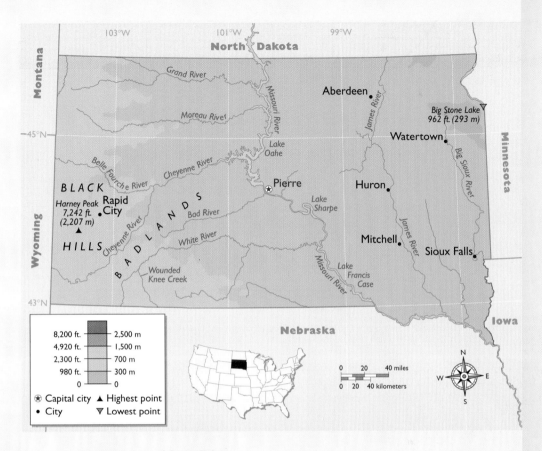

▲ **A topographic map of South Dakota**

other crops on this fertile **prairie.** The James and Big Sioux

Rivers run through East River. Sioux Falls lies on the banks

of the Big Sioux. Farther upstream is Watertown.

The land to the west of the Missouri River is known as

West River. Great herds of bison, or buffalo, once roamed

these rolling plains. Now cattle graze on the grasslands.

Buttes, or steep flat-topped hills, rise here and there. Pierre,

▲ The Badlands are home to many interesting rock formations.

the state capital, is in the center of the state. It's located on the Missouri River.

In the southwest are the Badlands. Why are the Badlands "bad"? The weather has given them a bad beating, making them hard to travel across. *Mako sica,* or "land bad," was what the Lakota Sioux called this area. Wind and rain lashed across this land for thousands of years. This swept away soil and left an unusual **wasteland.** Its ragged rock formations are orange, purple, and gray. The remains of many **prehistoric** animals have been found there.

In far western South Dakota are the Black Hills. Many caves, lakes, and canyons are in these forested hills. From a distance, the forests make the hills look black. Miners rushed here for gold in the late 1870s. Rapid City grew up as a miners' supply town.

The most famous peak in the Black Hills is Mount Rushmore. Four gigantic presidents' heads are carved into its rock face. Each face is 60 feet (18 meters) high. That's as high as a five-story building!

▲ Prospectors looking for gold at Rockerville, where $350,000 in gold was found between 1876 and 1878

▲ You can admire these awesome sculptures of Washington, Jefferson, Roosevelt, and Lincoln (left to right) at Mount Rushmore.

▲ Bison in Custer State Park

Elk, coyotes, and prairie dogs roam the hills and plains. Bobcats, pronghorns, and deer live in South Dakota, too. Bighorn sheep are sometimes seen on the rugged western terrain. Wild turkeys and pheasants find shelter in woods and tall grasses. Thousands of bison live in South Dakota today. They were almost wiped out from overhunting. Now they're protected by the government. The world's largest herd is in Custer State Park, near the town of Custer.

Summer in South Dakota can get very hot. The southeast is the warmest region. Sometimes the crops fail from lack of rain. Winter is cold, with temperatures often dropping below freezing. Temperatures are mild in the Black Hills. Winters are warmer there, and summers are cooler. Visitors can enjoy the Black Hills all year round.

▲ Snow blows across prairie grass in Bison Flats.

Thousands of Native Americans have always lived in South Dakota. The first Native American inhabitants of this area

▲ Rain-in-the-Face was a Hunkpapa Lakota Sioux warrior born near the Cheyenne River. He was involved in the Battle of the Little Bighorn in 1876.

were members of the Arikara and Cheyenne Nations. The Arikara lived in villages along the Missouri River. They were farmers who grew corn, beans, squash, and pumpkins. They traded their vegetables to the Cheyenne for buffalo meat and hides. The Cheyenne hunted buffalo across South Dakota's great plains. The Lakota, Dakota, and Nakota Sioux moved into South Dakota from Minnesota in the mid-1700s. Like the Cheyenne, the Sioux moved across the plains hunting buffalo.

Around this time, France claimed present-day South Dakota. In 1862, it became part of France's huge Louisiana **Colony.** The United States bought this land from France in 1803. President Thomas Jefferson sent Meriwether Lewis and William Clark to explore and map the area. The explorers passed through South Dakota in 1804 and again in 1806. Soon, fur traders began opening trading posts along South Dakota's rivers. In 1817, Joseph La Framboise opened a trading post on the Bad River. La Framboise's

▲ Fur trading posts like this one began developing along South Dakota's rivers during the early 1800s.

trading post became South Dakota's first permanent non-Native American settlement. It was located in the present-day town of Fort Pierre.

By the early 1800s, the Lakota, Dakota, and Nakota Sioux had driven out the Arikara and Cheyenne Nations. Wanting to preserve their traditional way of life, many Sioux **bands** signed peace treaties with the U.S. government. They moved to the largely unsettled western part of the state where the buffalo still roamed. Many white settlers and pioneers began moving into land left empty by the Sioux. The U.S. Congress created Dakota Territory in 1861. The Dakota Territory included North Dakota, South Dakota, and much of Wyoming and Montana.

In 1866, the U.S. Army began building a road to Montana's goldfields through the Sioux's western homelands. To protect their hunting grounds and sacred Black Hills, the Sioux, under Chief Red Cloud's leadership, fought the soldiers. The two-year war, known as Red Cloud's War, ended in 1868 with the signing of the Laramie Treaty. The treaty promised that the Sioux would remain the owners of the Black Hills area. Following the signing of the treaty, the Sioux moved west of the Missouri River.

In 1874, General George Armstrong Custer and army soldiers discovered gold in the Black Hills. Miners quickly followed and founded the towns of Deadwood and Rapid City. The mining towns were wild and lawless. Lawman Wild Bill Hickok moved in to clean up Deadwood. Things

▲ **To end Red Cloud's War, members of the Peace Commission met with Native American leaders.**

▲ **The Black Hills stagecoach at Deadwood**

didn't work out too well for Wild Bill, though. He was shot in the back and killed by gambler Jack McCall in 1876.

In the hopes of keeping newcomers off their land, Chiefs Crazy Horse and Sitting Bull led their people in many battles against the U.S. Army. In 1877, the U.S. government broke the Laramie Treaty and took ownership of the sacred Black Hills from the Sioux Nation. By 1889, most of the state's Sioux bands were living on **reservations.**

Many members of the Sioux continued to hope for a return of their traditional way of life. They often participated in prayers and religious ceremonies, like the Ghost Dance ceremony, in the hopes of bringing about this return. The U.S. government misunderstood the Ghost Dance ceremony and feared that the Sioux were planning a violent uprising. The army was sent in. On December 29, 1890, they fired on a group of Sioux gathered at Wounded Knee Creek. About three hundred Sioux men, women, and children were

▲ Tokens adorning a memorial at Wounded Knee Creek, the site of the Wounded Knee Massacre

murdered that day. The tragic event is known as the Wounded Knee Massacre.

With the introduction of the railroad to South Dakota in the 1870s and 1880s, more farmers, cattle ranchers, and gold miners arrived. New towns sprang up at the railroad stops. In 1889, South Dakota became the fortieth U.S. state.

South Dakotans suffered terrible droughts, or lack of rain. A drought in the 1890s lasted for years. Another drought struck in 1911. The 1930s brought drought, dust

▲ Many towns and railroad stations like these began to fill up the Great Plains in the 1880s.

storms, and grasshopper **invasions.** At the same time, the Great Depression swept the nation. Thousands of South Dakotans lost their farms and homes. The U.S. government helped with job projects. They built roads, bridges, and schools. During World War II (1939–1945), several army bases opened in South Dakota.

After the war, many South Dakotans left the state. Farming was suffering, and they needed to find jobs. The state began building large dams on the Missouri River. The dams

▲ Grasshoppers covered the window screen of this farmer's house. Millions more devoured his crops.

created lakes and controlled floods. They also provided water-powered electricity and irrigation water.

South Dakota's Sioux still remembered the U.S. government taking their sacred Black Hills. In 1973, they occupied the village of Wounded Knee for seventy-one days. The U.S. government offered payment to the Sioux for the Black Hills in 1980, but the Sioux didn't take the money. They wanted their land. The dispute continues to this day.

▲ The Big Bend Dam at Fort Thompson created energy for the state.

▲ Richard Wilson, president of the Oglala Sioux Tribal Council, shows the names of Native American activists charged by the U.S. government with unlawful activities at Wounded Knee in 1973.

South Dakota's farmers still struggle to make a living. Meanwhile, tourism is a growing industry. Visitors love South Dakota's historic sites and haunting **landscape.**

The capitol in Pierre

Pierre is South Dakota's capital city. It's the center of the state's government. South Dakota's government works much like the U.S. government. It's divided into three branches—legislative, executive, and judicial.

The legislative branch makes the state laws. South Dakota voters choose lawmakers to serve in the state's legislature. The legislature is divided into two houses, or parts. One is the thirty-five-member senate. The other is the seventy-member house of representatives. They all meet in January at the state capitol in Pierre.

The executive branch carries out the state's laws. South Dakota's governor is the head of the executive branch. The state's voters elect a governor every four years. He or she may serve only two terms in a row. Voters also elect many other executive officers.

The judicial branch is made up of judges and their courts. The judges are experts when it comes to South Dakota's laws. They decide whether a person or group has broken the law. South Dakota's highest court is the five-member state supreme court.

▲ **The Minnehaha County Courthouse in Sioux Falls**

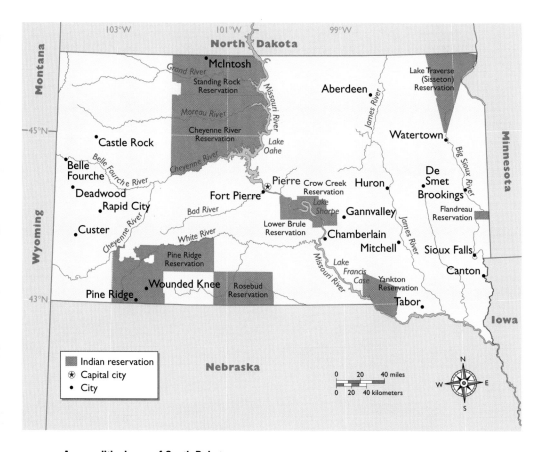

▲ **A geopolitical map of South Dakota**

South Dakota is divided into sixty-six counties. Voters in each county elect county commissioners. South Dakota's cities and towns have home rule. That means they can choose their own form of government. Most elect a mayor and a city council.

South Dakota's Native Americans have their own tribal government. Residents on each reservation elect a chairperson, vice chairperson, secretary, and treasurer. They also elect members to the tribal council. Council members meet with their communities every month. All the tribes send representatives to meet once a year with the National Sioux Council. The reservations also have a court system.

▲ Lakota leaders on the Pine Ridge Reservation presented Commissioner John Collier with the gift of a pipe in 1934. Through the Indian Reorganization Act, Collier helped tribal groups form constitutional governments and protect reservation lands.

Gainesboro Elementary School
Winchester, Virginia

Miners once swarmed over the Black Hills searching for gold. South Dakota was a leading gold-mining state. In 2000, it was the sixth-highest gold-producing state. Homestake Mine was the largest gold mine in the **Americas.** It closed in 2001 after operating for 125 years. A national science laboratory will be taking its place and filling its underground tunnels.

▲ **A gold-mining pit in Lead**

▲ Soybean crop rows in Turner County

After gold, iron ore and silver are the leading metals. Other important minerals are sand, gravel, limestone, and granite. South Dakota ranks second in granite dimension stone. That's granite that can be removed in large blocks.

South Dakota's farmers have always been tough. They've lived through droughts, dust storms, and insect swarms. Today, the state's farmers are still tough. Farms and ranches

▲ A cowboy moves cattle across the prairie near Chamberlain.

cover most of South Dakota. Fields spread across the eastern half of the state. Farmers there grow corn, soybeans, wheat, and other crops. Some also raise hogs and dairy cows. South Dakota ranks second only to North Dakota in the production of sunflowers and flaxseed. It's third in hay, rye, and honey, and fourth in oats.

Western South Dakota is cattle country. Beef cattle are the most valuable farm animals. They graze across vast stretches of grassy prairie. Ranchers also raise sheep. South Dakota is the fourth-ranking state in sheep and lambs. Sheep's wool is an important farm product.

South Dakota's leading factory goods are computers and other electronics. Next in value are processed foods. Many food plants process meat. Others make dairy products from milk. The state also produces heavy equipment for farming and construction.

Service workers in South Dakota hold many jobs. They may sell homes, care for the sick, or repair motorcycles. Some work in banks or other money-related businesses. Others work in national parks, Native American reservations, schools, or the tourism and hospitality industries.

▲ The Gateway computer company assembly warehouse in North Sioux City

In 2000, there were 754,844 people in South Dakota. Only four other states have a smaller population. About half the residents live in city areas. The largest cities are Sioux Falls, Rapid City, and Aberdeen. Pierre, the state capital, has fewer than fourteen thousand people.

Eight out of every nine South Dakotans are white. They belong to many ethnic groups. The largest groups come from Scandinavian countries—Norway, Sweden, or Denmark. Germans and German-Russians are another large group. Others have roots in Finland, the Netherlands, Ireland, England, or Wales.

One out of twelve South Dakota residents is Native American. Most are of Sioux descent. Many live on one of the state's nine reservations.

▲ Sioux Indians perform a traditional ceremony on the Rosebud Reservation.

▲ **This parade in Deadwood is part of the Days of '76 Festival.**

The Great Sioux Nation is divided into seven council fires or bands. The people of the Great Sioux Nation speak one of three languages—Dakota, Nakota, or Lakota. The largest number of them are of Lakota descent. Some **Hispanics,** Asians, and African-Americans live in South Dakota, too.

Many festivals celebrate South Dakotans' history and culture. The Black Hills Roundup is a big rodeo in Belle Fourche. The Days of '76 Festival in Deadwood celebrates the gold rush. Deadwood also presents a summer-long play, *The Trial of Jack McCall.* McCall was the man who killed Wild Bill Hickok.

Czech Days, held every June in Tabor, celebrates the culture of South Dakota's Czech settlers. People dance to polka music and feast on *kolache* pastries. In September, the Northern Plains Tribal Arts Festival is held in Sioux Falls.

People from the thirty-three Northern Plains tribes display their art. In October, Rapid City holds a similar festival. It's the Black Hills Powwow, which includes traditional dancing and arts. The Oglala Nation Fair and Powwow is in Pine Ridge in August. It's famous for its traditional dancing and drumming.

Author Laura Ingalls Wilder lived in De Smet. Some of her books describe children's lives during the pio-

▲ A member of the Cheyenne River Lakota tribe in traditional dress

▲ Laura Ingalls Wilder spent part of her childhood at this homestead in De Smet.

neer days there. *Little Town on the Prairie* tells about her school days and friends. *The Long Winter* is the story of how heavy snows created big problems for the Ingalls family. Author Ole Rölvaag lived in Canton, South Dakota. He later wrote about the rough lives of Norwegian pioneers. They were one of many groups whose hard work built South Dakota.

Suppose you had to carve faces into a mountain. How would you do it? Gutzon Borglum had the same problem when he was asked to carve four presidents' faces into

▲ A statue of the Oglala Lakota Sioux leader Crazy Horse is being carved into the Black Hills.

Mount Rushmore. He figured out how, though. Borglum did most of his job with **dynamite!** He knew just where to make it explode. Then, for a fine finish, he used air hammers. Today, Mount Rushmore is South Dakota's most famous site.

Another great monument, 600 feet (185 m) high, is being carved into the Black Hills. It's the Crazy Horse Memorial. When completed, it will be the world's largest sculpture. It honors the famous Oglala Lakota Sioux chief

▲ **You can see remains of mammoths at Mammoth Site in Hot Springs.**

Crazy Horse. He fought bravely to defend and preserve the Black Hills area for the Lakota Sioux people.

Many caves lie within the Black Hills. In Wind Cave, you can explore miles of winding paths. You'll see rare rock patterns called boxwork. They're thin strands of rock in a honeycomb design. You'll also see cave popcorn, which are popcorn-shaped rock clusters that sometimes form on cave walls.

Imagine a shaggy elephant that stands taller than your bedroom. That's what mammoths looked like. Scientists found hundreds of these **prehistoric** animals at Mammoth Site in Hot Springs. Scientists are still digging there today. You can watch them at work and tour the museum.

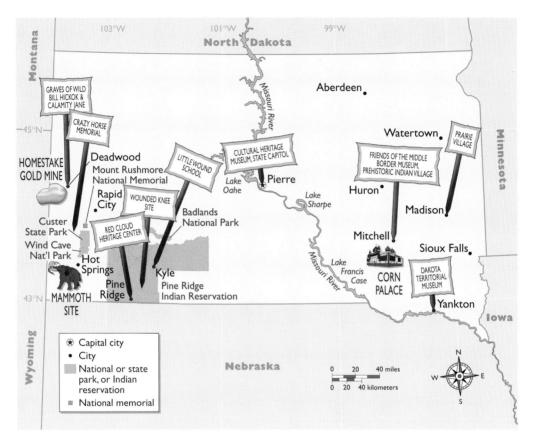

Places to visit in South Dakota

Deadwood was once a wild mining town. It still has a **frontier** flavor. Deadwood's Mount Moriah Cemetery has some famous "residents." One is Wild Bill Hickok. Another is Calamity Jane. Calamity means disaster. As you can guess, she was a rowdy frontier woman.

The Cultural Heritage Museum is in Pierre. There you'll explore pioneer life, mining days, Native Americans, and much more. Nearby is the state capitol. From Pierre, you can head out to the Great Lakes of South Dakota. They were formed by four dams on the Missouri River. They're great spots for boating, fishing, swimming, and camping.

▲ **A family enjoys a sunny day on Sylvan Lake in Custer State Park.**

You've never seen anything like Mitchell's gigantic Corn Palace! It's covered inside and out with artwork made from corn and other grains. Near Mitchell is the Prehistoric

▲ The Corn Palace in Mitchell is decorated with corn, grain, and grasses grown in South Dakota.

Indian Village. Its exhibits include arrowheads, tools, and a life-sized earth lodge.

Pioneer days come alive at Yankton's Dakota Territorial Museum. You'll see the blacksmith shop, schoolhouse, and other buildings from the 1800s. You can also explore frontier life at many other sites. One is the Friends of the Middle Border Museum in Mitchell. Another is Madison's Prairie Village, which has more than forty historic buildings.

The Badlands are truly a wonderland. You'll wander among tall, pointy rocks and colorful cliffs. One area has a prairie dog town. You may also see coyotes, pronghorns, bighorn sheep, and bison. Scientists are currently trying to reintroduce the black-footed ferret to the Badlands. It is the most endangered land mammal in North America. Wounded Knee Creek is also in the Badlands. A small marker shows where its Sioux victims are buried.

Red Cloud Heritage Center is in nearby Pine Ridge. The Pine Ridge Reservation is the largest in the state. Lakota Sioux children attend Little Wound School in Kyle. The school has its own living history village. Children

▲ The scenic falls of the Big Sioux River in Sioux Falls

demonstrate traditional songs, dances, and crafts there. They are happy to share their culture with visitors.

Sioux Falls was one of the first towns in South Dakota. If you visit, you can tour the historic mill and admire beautiful falls on the Big Sioux River.

While you watch the rough water move past the old mill, think of the rugged people of this land. Their spirit is one of the many things that makes South Dakota great!

Important Dates

1743 French explorers Francois and Louis-Joseph La Verendrye are the first Europeans in South Dakota.

1803 South Dakota passes to the United States in the Louisiana Purchase.

1804, 1806 Meriwether Lewis and William Clark explore South Dakota.

1817 Joseph La Framboise makes South Dakota's first permanent non-Native American settlement at present-day Fort Pierre.

1861 Dakota Territory is created.

1868 Red Cloud's War ends with the Laramie Treaty; the Sioux are promised the Black Hills.

1874 General George Armstrong Custer and army soldiers discover gold in the Black Hills.

1889 South Dakota becomes the fortieth state on November 2.

1890 More than three hundred Lakota Sioux are murdered at Wounded Knee Creek on December 29.

1927 Gutzon Borglum begins the Mount Rushmore National Memorial.

1939 Badlands National Park is created.

1973 Members of the American Indian Movement occupy the village of Wounded Knee to protest broken treaties and discrimination.

1980 The U.S. government offers to pay the Sioux for land it took in 1877.

1989 South Dakota celebrates its centennial with a real wagon train that travels 2,614 miles (4,207 kilometers) throughout the state in four months.

2003 Construction continues on the Crazy Horse Memorial in the Black Hills. Workers are uncertain as to when the monument will be completed.

Glossary

Americas—the lands of the Western Hemisphere, including North, Central, and South America and the West Indies

bands—groups of people joined together for a common purpose because of a shared culture

colony—a territory that belongs to the country that settles it

dynamite—a material that makes a powerful explosion

frontier—unexplored land

Hispanic—people of Mexican, South American, and other Spanish-speaking cultures

invasions—unwanted entries into someone's territory

landscape—a view of a large area of land

monument—a large structure built in honor of a person or event

prairie—level or rolling grassland

prehistoric—occurring before people began recording history

reservations—large areas of land set aside for Native Americans

wasteland—land that is barren, empty, or ruined

Did You Know?

★ It took Gutzon Borglum and his son, Lincoln, more than fourteen years to complete the sculptures on Mount Rushmore. Washington's head was completed first. Next came Jefferson, Lincoln, and then Roosevelt.

★ The geographical center of the United States is in western South Dakota. If you drew a north-south line and an east-west line across the country (including Alaska and Hawaii) and centered them, they would meet 17 miles (27 km) west of Castle Rock.

★ Badlands National Park contains fossils that are 35 million years old.

★ The Lakota Sioux gave the Black Hills their name. They called the hills *Paha Sapa,* which means "black hills."

★ Harney Peak, in the Black Hills, is the highest point in the United States east of the Rocky Mountains.

State capital: Pierre

State motto: Under God the People Rule

State slogan: Great Faces, Great Places

State nickname: Mount Rushmore State

Statehood: November 2, 1889; fortieth state

Land area: 77,122 square miles (199,746 sq km); **rank:** sixteenth

Highest point: Harney Peak, 7,242 feet (2,207 m)

Lowest point: Big Stone Lake, 962 feet (293 m) above sea level

Highest recorded temperature: 120°F (49°C) at Gannvalley on July 5, 1936

Lowest recorded temperature: −58°F (−50°C) at McIntosh on February 17, 1936

Average January temperature: 16°F (−9°C)

Average July temperature: 74°F (23°C)

Population in 2000: 754,844; **rank:** forty-sixth

Largest cities in 2000: Sioux Falls (123,975), Rapid City (59,607), Aberdeen (24,658), Watertown (20,237)

Factory products: Computers and electronics, food products, machinery

Farm products: Beef cattle, corn, hay, hogs, milk, oats, rye, sorghum, sunflowers, soybeans, wheat, sheep, honey

Mining products: Gold, crushed stone, sand and gravel, petroleum

State flag: South Dakota's state flag shows the state seal upon a field of blue. Golden rays of the sun surround the seal. Around the rays are the words "South Dakota, The Mount Rushmore State." That's the state's official nickname.

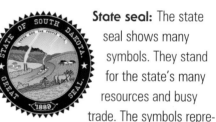

State seal: The state seal shows many symbols. They stand for the state's many resources and busy trade. The symbols represent South Dakota's farming, ranching, industries, lumbering, manufacturing, and mining. Above them is a banner with the state motto, "Under God the People Rule." At the bottom is the date 1889, the year of statehood.

State abbreviations: S.Dak. or S.D. (traditional); SD (postal)

State Symbols

State bird: Chinese ring-necked pheasant

State flower: American pasque flower (May Day flower)

State tree: Black Hills spruce

State animal: Coyote

State fish: Walleye

State insect: Honey bee

State mineral: Rose quartz

State gemstone: Fairburn agate

State jewelry: Black Hills gold

State soil: Houdek soil

State fossil: *Triceratops*

State greeting: *"How Kola!"* (Hello, Friend!)

State dessert: Kuchen

Making Apple Kuchen

Kuchen is South Dakota's delicious state dessert.

Makes twenty to twenty-four servings.

INGREDIENTS:

Crust:

2 cups flour

1/2 cup sugar

1/4 teaspoon Kosher salt

2 sticks of unsalted butter

1/2 teaspoon vanilla extract

Filling:

1 pound cream cheese, room temperature

3/4 cup sugar

1 teaspoon vanilla extract

1 egg

Topping:

3 Granny Smith apples, peeled, cored, and sliced

2 tablespoons sugar

1 1/2 teaspoons cinnamon

DIRECTIONS:

Make sure an adult helps you with the hot stove and the cutting. Preheat the oven to 450°F. Grease and flour a 9-by-13-inch pan. For the crust, mix flour, sugar, and salt in a large bowl. Cut the butter into pieces. Add butter and vanilla to the bowl and mix. Press into pan and bake 12 to 15 minutes. Let it cool. Turn the oven down to 400°F. For the filling, mix the cream cheese, sugar, and vanilla until creamy. Mix in the egg. Pour into the cooled crust. For the topping, place apple slices evenly across the top. Mix sugar and cinnamon and sprinkle over the apples. Bake until firm and brown, about 20 minutes. Cut into twenty to twenty-four pieces. Serve warm, adding ice cream on top if you like.

"Hail, South Dakota"

Words and music by DeeCort Hammitt

Hail! South Dakota, A great state of the land,
Health, wealth and beauty, That's what makes her grand;
She has her Black Hills, And mines with gold so rare,
And with her scenery, No other state can compare.

Come where the sun shines, And where life's worth your while,
You won't be here long, 'Till you'll wear a smile.
No state's so healthy, and no folk quite so true,
To South Dakota. We welcome you.

Hail! South Dakota, The state we love the best,
Land of our fathers, Builders of the west;
Home of the Badlands, and Rushmore's ageless shrine,
Black Hills and prairies, Farmland and Sunshine.
Hills, farms and prairies, Blessed with bright Sunshine.

Gutzon Borglum (1867–1941) created the sculptures of presidents' faces on Mount Rushmore. He was born in Idaho.

Tom Brokaw (1940–) is a television news reporter. He hosts the *NBC Nightly News.*

Amanda Clement (1888–1971) was the first woman paid to umpire a baseball game. In 1964, she was inducted into the South Dakota Hall of Fame.

Crazy Horse (1849?–1877) was an Oglala Sioux chief. He defended the Black Hills and fought in Montana's Battle of the Little Bighorn. He defeated General George Crook at the Battle of Rosebud Creek.

Tom Daschle (1947–) became a U.S. senator from South Dakota in 1987. He is a Democratic Party leader in Congress.

Hubert H. Humphrey Jr. (1911–1978) was a U.S. senator from Minnesota. A Democrat, he served as vice president under Lyndon Johnson (1965–1969). He ran for president in 1968 but lost.

Cheryl Ladd (1951–) is an actress. She starred in the television series *Charlie's Angels* and many movies.

George McGovern (1922–) was a U.S. senator from South Dakota (1963–1981). In 1972, he ran as the Democratic candidate for president but lost.

Red Cloud (1822–1909) was the Oglala Sioux chief who led Red Cloud's War. He had hoped the Laramie Treaty would protect his people's hunting grounds.

Ole Rölvaag (1876–1931) was a novelist who lived for a time in Canton. His novels tell about the hard lives of Norwegian pioneers in America. *Giants in the Earth, Peder Victorious,* and *Their Father's God* is his trilogy, or three-novel set. He was born in Norway and taught in Minnesota.

Sitting Bull (1831–1890) was a Hunkpapa Lakota chief and spiritual leader. Sitting Bull (pictured above left) led his people against General Custer at the Battle of the Little Bighorn in Montana.

Spotted Tail (1823?–1881) was a Brulé Sioux leader. He signed the Laramie Treaty of 1868. Later, he took part in selling the Black Hills to help secure food for his tribe.

Laura Ingalls Wilder (1867–1957) wrote many children's books. *The Long Winter, Little Town on the Prairie,* and *By the Shores of Silver Lake* tell about her time in De Smet. She was born in Wisconsin.

Want to Know More?

At the Library

Latza, Jodi, and Greg Latza (photographer). *South Dakota: An Alphabetical Scrapbook.* Sioux Falls, S.Dak.: PeopleScapes, Inc., 2000.

Left Hand Bull, Jacqueline, and Suzanne Haldane (illustrator). *Lakota Hoop Dancer.* New York: Dutton Books, 1999.

Rose, LaVera. *Grandchildren of the Lakota.* Minneapolis: CarolRhoda Books, 1998.

Shepherd, Donna Walsh. *South Dakota.* Danbury, Conn.: Children's Press, 2001.

Thompson, Kathleen. *South Dakota.* Austin, Tex.: Raintree/Steck-Vaughn, 1996.

Welsbacher, Anne. *South Dakota.* Edina, Minn.: Abdo & Daughters, 1998.

Wilder, Laura Ingalls, and Garth Williams (illustrator). *Little Town on the Prairie.* New York: HarperCollins, 1987.

Wilder, Laura Ingalls, and Garth Williams (illustrator). *The Long Winter.* New York: HarperCollins, 1987.

On the Web
South Dakota Home Page
http://www.state.sd.us/
To learn about South Dakota's history, government, economy, and land

South Dakota Travel
http://www.travelsd.com
To find out about South Dakota's events, activities, and sights

Through the Mail
South Dakota Department of Tourism
Capitol Lake Plaza
711 East Wells Avenue
Pierre, SD 57501
For information on travel and interesting sights in South Dakota

South Dakota State Historical Society
Department of Education and Cultural Affairs
Cultural Heritage Center
900 Governors Drive
Pierre, SD 57501
For information on South Dakota's history

On the Road
South Dakota State Capitol
500 East Capitol Avenue
Pierre, SD 57501
605/773-3765
To visit South Dakota's state capitol

Index

About the Author

Ann Heinrichs grew up in Fort Smith, Arkansas, and lives in Chicago. She is the author of more than one hundred books for children and young adults on Asian, African, and U.S. history and culture. Ann has also written numerous newspaper, magazine, and encyclopedia articles. She is an award-winning martial artist, specializing in t'ai chi empty-hand and sword forms.

Ann has traveled widely throughout the United States, Africa, Asia, and the Middle East. In exploring each state for this series, she rediscovered the people, history, and resources that make this a great land, as well as the concerns we share with people around the world.